IMAGES OF MINISTRY

Reflections Of A
Seminary President

HERMAN G. STUEMPFLE, JR.

CSS Publishing Company, Inc.
Lima, Ohio

IMAGES OF MINISTRY

Copyright © 1995 by
CSS Publishing Company, Inc.
Lima, Ohio

All rights reserved. No part of this publication may be reproduced in any manner whatsoever without prior permission of the publisher, except in the case of brief quotations embodied in critical articles and reviews. Inquiries should be addressed to: Permissions, CSS Publishing Company, Inc., 517 South Main Street, P.O. Box 4503, Lima, Ohio 45802-4503.

Scripture quotations are from the *New Revised Standard Version of the Bible,* copyright 1989, by the Division of Christian Education of the National Council of the Churches of Christ in the USA. Used by permission.

Scripture quotations are from the *Revised Standard Version of the Bible,* copyrighted 1946, 1952 (c), 1971, 1973, by the Division of Christian Education of the National Council of the Churches of Christ in the USA. Used by permission.

Scripture quotations are from *The New English Bible,* copyright (c) the Delegates of the Oxford University Press and the Syndics of the Cambridge University Press, 1961, 1970. Reprinted by permission.

Library of Congress Cataloging-in-Publication Data

Stuempfle, Herman G.
   Images of ministry / Herman G. Stuempfle, Jr.
     p.   cm.
   ISBN 0-7880-0575-8
   1. Clergy—Office. I. Title.
BV660.2.S84   1995
253—dc20   95-13426
                                                                                     CIP

ISBN 0-7880-0575-8   PRINTED IN U.S.A.

Not only is the preacher a husband to his congregation: he is an archer, a watchman, a trumpeter, a harmonious charmer; he possesses the most desirable qualities of a lion, an ox, an eagle, and a man; he is an earthquake, a son of thunder, the fall of waters, the roaring of a lion.

— in William R. Mueller,
John Donne: Preacher, p. 43.

Contents

Preface 7

Clay Pots 9

Broken Vessels 15

Thieves 19

Waiters 23

Stars 29

Poets 33

Spies 37

Nightwatchers 43

Fools 49

Survivors 53

Sowers 59

Christ's Militia 65

Preface

It is a truism that our self-image conditions the quality and effectiveness of our lives. The metaphors by which we characteristically define ourselves — loser, winner, victim, lover, beloved — reach faithful expression in attitude and behavior. When persons enter therapy, a major goal is often to alter the image of the self. The intent is to displace unhelpful or even destructive metaphors of being with images of the self which will issue in more free and productive lives.

Those of us who are engaged in church ministries also function under the power of images. The church's ancient tradition offers a generous array of possibilities, among them such familiar models as prophet, priest, pastor or deacon. The contemporary church adds others — counselor, enabler, manager. Some question whether the older images still have relevance. Others doubt that the newer ones are sufficiently rooted in the gospel of which we are called to be servants.

It is my purpose in this book to offer another set of images for our public ministries. A few are recognizable as variations on some of the traditional images. Others are less conventional and may strike the reader as odd. Certainly no one of them nor indeed any combination of them is a sufficient metaphor for the complex, many faceted task to which we are called. I hope that each reader will find them catalytic for her or his own reflections on ministry.

If readers detect in these pages echoes of the spoken word, they will not be mistaken. All but one of these chapters first saw the light of day as, in one case, a sermon and as, in the rest, addresses to graduating classes at the seminary I was privileged to serve. They are united, I trust, by their references to now one aspect and now another of our special ministries among the people of God.

This last sentence leads me to a final observation. In writing specifically about special ministries in the church, I am by no means unmindful of the broader New Testament understanding of ministry. A central concern across nearly a half century of ordained ministry has been the envisioning and the liberating of the ministry of all the baptized people of God. "Ministry" is for me an "omnibus word," carrying references to the ordained and those in other full-time offices, but, more fundamentally, inclusive of all who are part of the Body of Christ. Though I am offering images through which pastors and those whom we unhelpfully call "lay professionals" may view their work, I hope that much that follows will be of use also to that immense body of the laity who fulfill their ministries primarily in structures outside the church. In fact, the final chapter of the book, originally a sermon to a local congregation, lifts up an image for ministry in which those whose "stations" are in the world have the largest place. Their general ministry in daily life is always the context and the objective of our special ministries in the church.

It is customary for authors to express appreciation to those whose help has been part of the making of a book. In this case, that pleasant task would be impossible. Their name is "Legion" — colleagues and students, family and friends who, across the years, have shaped my understanding of ministry and have supported, corrected and stimulated me in its exercise. I hope some of them will hear their voices and recognize their fingerprints in the pages that follow.

I dedicate this book to my children, Stephen, David and Kristin, each of whom has ministered to me through his or her unique person and gifts.

Herman G. Stuempfle, Jr.
Gettysburg, Pennsylvania

Clay Pots

Having a son who's a working potter has given me a new appreciation for that ancient craft. It still appears to me to be a form of magic. A lump of formless clay is plopped on a spinning wheel and then, under gentle pressure from the hands of the potter, rises upward in defiance of all the laws of gravity and finally takes on a beautiful shape.

Watching that artistic marvel occur has also given me a new ear with which to hear what the biblical writers have to say about clay and potters and pots. There's a surprising amount of it, some of it factual, more of it metaphorical. For example, there's Jeremiah's famous visit to a Jerusalem potter. He sees the potter throw a pot, express his displeasure at the result, squash the soft clay pot down again and then throw another more to his liking. For Jeremiah it's a sermon illustration: "O house of Israel, can I not do with you as the potter has done? says the Lord. Behold, like the clay in the potter's hand, so are you in my hand, O house of Israel" (Jeremiah 18:16).

Then, jumping across the centuries, there's Saint Paul's familiar characterization of the apostolic ministry: "... we have this treasure (the gospel) in earthen vessels ..." (2 Corinthians 4:7a). A less elegant but more literal translation of the final words would be "in clay pots."

As is the case with all metaphors, this one isn't perfect. For one thing, clay is inanimate. It isn't quite the right symbol, therefore, for us living, thinking, feeling, yearning, rebelling creatures who are called to ministry. Isaiah makes use of this discrepancy between analogy and analog in his ironic question. "Does the clay say to the one who fashions it, 'What are you making?' or, 'Your work has no handles' " (Isaiah 45:9b). Of course not!

Yet granted its limitations as a total image for ministry, this good, earthy biblical language of clay and pots and potters has its uses as we reflect on our various ministries in the church.

Because so much of my ministry was in theological education, I see some implications for the seminaries of the church. If the church's ministers are clay pots, then it follows that its seminaries are potteries. They certainly can't and don't claim ultimate responsibility for the shape in which their "products" emerge from the kiln, but, at least in some penultimate way, seminary faculties have had their foot on the wheel and their hand in the clay. For better or worse, the church's pastors and lay ministers go out into the church bearing the stamp of their crafting.

Seminaries, at their best, will resist becoming "mass production" potteries. They won't pour all their students into the same mold, so that they come out in standard form, like the mugs on display in a tourist shop. Rather, like serious artists, seminary faculties will work to form their students in a way both consistent with the church's design (read "tradition") and respectful of each student's uniqueness. How well they succeed is never immediately clear. The real test comes only with years of actual ministerial service by those who confess with Saint Paul: "... we have this treasure in clay pots ...."

* * *

One thing this image suggests is that our creation as vessels of the gospel is not of our own choosing. There's no clay pot until the potter decides to make one. And there's no minister, lay or ordained, in the church until God, in God's own way and in God's good time, decides there shall be one.

No amount of autobiographical, sociological or psychological analysis can solve the infinitely complex riddle of why those who serve the church as its leaders are where they are. I know all about the influence of "significant others" — family, friends, pastors, teachers. I know about the impact of critical events — marriages, deaths, traumas, defeats. I know the importance of doors which inexplicably open and sometimes just as inexplicably close. I know too that it's finally the church which calls us into ministry. There's no end to the traceable human factors which bring us, sometimes kicking and screaming, sometimes with indescribable relief, into our special callings. But "in, with and under" all these identifiable human factors, faith discerns the hand of the Eternal Potter who silently, relentlessly shapes the raw clay of our lives into a pot which will hold the priceless treasure of the gospel.

The process begins when our clay is mixed with Water and Word at the font. The Spirit's shaping continues through all the years prior to our ordination or commissioning and extends to the end of our days. Most often that shaping Hand is hidden from our eyes. Indeed, the strains and conflicts of our ministries and the painful awareness of our inadequacies can undermine our confidence that a Potter is anywhere in sight, let alone at work. We can only cling in faith to the promise: "You did not choose me, but I chose you" (John 15:16). No matter how we may feel at any given moment, the truth stands: "We are the clay, and you are the potter" (Isaiah 64:18). It is you, Lord, who have formed me from my mother's womb and, for your own strange and indecipherable reasons, have shaped me into a vessel for your gospel!

* * *

It can also help us to remember that a potter doesn't require perfect clay in order to make a good pot. Certainly a serious potter tries to get hold of the best clay she or he can find. Otherwise it would be a waste of time and artistry and a fraud upon those to whom the pots are eventually sold. Therefore, the skill of the potter can never be turned into a rationalization for adding carelessness or neglect to the deficient raw material we already are! I think often of words H.H. Farmer wrote many years ago about the task of preaching: "God may indeed use the foolishness of preaching, but we are under obligation to see that it is not more foolish than it need be."[1]

So, to say that God doesn't require *perfect* clay to turn us into sturdy, functional pots for carrying the gospel to the church, doesn't mean that God isn't interested in *good* clay. That's why, on our journey into ministry, we have to run the gauntlet of admissions standards, graduation requirements and examination by some ecclesiastical body. It's all part of the church's concern to see, insofar as humanly possible, that the clay placed in God's hands for shaping into a vessel for the gospel is no more inadequate than it need be. But having said that, the principle still holds: God doesn't require perfect clay to make a good pot.

Through a half century of ministry, I've found that axiom to be a comfort and an encouragement. Wherever ministry takes us, hardly a day will go by when we won't be aware that the Potter could have chosen a bigger, better or more graceful vessel for bearing the gospel to that part of the church in which we find ourselves. It isn't only that our *feet* are clay; the whole of our humanity is! But, as Nikos Kazantzakis once wrote, "God is a potter; he works in mud."[2]

What's even harder, however, are the days when the vessel isn't just too obviously clay, but when it's broken. Pottery is a good bit tougher than it looks, my son tells me, but it isn't shatter-proof. And there come moments when our life and ministry seem to disintegrate into jagged shards. A crisis erupts in the parish and shatters the fragile networks of trust and love that have been years in the making. Or, we're overtaken by — perhaps contribute to — calamity that seems to call into question every word of truth and hope we've preached. What do we do when the pot of clay lies all in pieces and the wine of the gospel appears to be vanishing into the earth?

I can only say that it's at this point, above all others, that our metaphor breaks down. It's impossible for a potter to turn brittle shards into clay again and shape them into a new pot. But, thank God, we are not lifeless clay. And, thank God, we're held in the hands of no ordinary potter. The God who has chosen us is that Artist of the Impossible who took a shattered body from a cross and transformed it into a life of deathless love and infinite power. Only *therefore* can we say with Saint Paul:

> *But we have this treasure in clay pots, to show that the transcendent power belongs to God and not to us.*

---

1. H.H. Farmer. *The Servant Of The Word* (James Nisbet & Co. Ltd.: Welwyn, 1941), p. 30.

2. Nikos Kazantzakis. *The Greek Passion* (Simon and Schuster: New York, 1965), p. 151.

Broken Vessels

I want to begin by asking what may at first seem an odd question: "Can a Christian be a pastor?" Or, the order of the nouns might be reversed and the question asked this way: "Can a pastor, or other office holder in the church, be a Christian?"

A version of such questions was once pressed upon me by back-to-back experiences. The first was a reading of Frederick Buechner's novel, *The Final Beast*. The novel's central character is a beleaguered young clergyman, the Reverend Theodore Nicolet. About him I will say more later.

The second experience was that of moderating a symposium on professional ethics, particularly in the fields of business, medicine and law. The lawyer on the panel posed the question for his profession in exactly the form in which I've amended it for ours: "Can a Christian be a lawyer?"

Actually there's a long history of people asking such questions about the station they or others occupy in this world. Jesus' disciples asked it one day about persons of wealth: "Can a rich man enter the kingdom of heaven?" Luther once devoted a whole tract to a similar query about the military: "Can soldiers also be saved?" If we really do believe in "the priesthood of all believers" and view professional ministry as a particular office in that general priesthood of the faithful, then there's no good reason why we should be exempt from asking that same kind of question about ourselves: "Can a Christian be a pastor or a lay professional in the church?"

No doubt our immediate and instinctive answer is, "Why, of course! What an absurd question! Aren't we, after all, the 'representative Christians' in the midst of the church?" I once heard a high ranking denominational official, in the course of installing a lay person into a full-time church position, comment: "Now he's an example of what every Christian should aspire to be." His observation was uncomfortably close in spirit to Luther's lightning-flash induced decision to become a monk to save his soul, a delusion whose cure was, in many respects, a source of the Reformation.

A similar point of view is sometimes expressed by "second career" inquirers who appear on a seminary campus. In the course of conversation they acknowledge that one reason they're considering full-time ministry in the church is to escape what they've discovered to be the ethically compromising milieu of some secular occupation. The only question is how long it will be before they lose their innocence. What will be their reaction when they find that the ecclesiastical realm, far from being a safe haven for the soul, is electric with new dangers?

Anyone who has been in ministry for any length of time can easily produce a list of those danger points: the moment we're tempted to compromise the integrity of the gospel for the sake of superficial harmony in the congregation; the moment we find ourselves proclaiming, "I believe," without any sense of the necessity to pray with equal fervor, "Lord, help my unbelief!"; the moment we begin to think of ourselves as "masters in the house" rather than "servants of the servants of God"; the moment we no longer see the comic absurdity that we, of all unholy people, are occupying a holy office; the moment we rationalize neglect of our families by pleading the demands of "the Lord's work"; and the moment we begin to think of our individual ministries as necessary for the church and the kingdom and forget that with God we're always on provisional assignment.

These are only a few of the danger points that suggest that the question, "Can a Christian also be a pastor or lay professional?" is by no means an issue settled in advance, any more than it is for the rich person, the soldier or the lawyer.

* * *

But now to return to those back-to-back experiences which prompted this question. The lawyer who posed it for his profession acknowledged that for him there could be no final and absolute answer. He had discovered he could only live with the question by keeping it open. To put it theologically, he had learned that there was no way he could justify himself in advance.

I'm convinced that this is no less true for those of us in professional ministry. The most useful (not necessarily successful) pastors I've known over the years are those for whom their right to be and remain in ministry is always to some degree an unsettled issue, a contingent arrangement, a question still to be resolved. Jesus' answer to the disciples about the possibility of salvation for a rich man could just as easily have been spoken to us whose riches are more likely to be "religious" or ecclesiastical than material:

> *It is easier for a camel to pass through the eye of a needle than for a rich man to enter the Kingdom of God. ... For men it is impossible, but not for God; everything is possible for God" (Mark 10:25-27).*

Like the kingdom itself, our callings within its life are an eschatological promise as well as a present task.

* * *

And now back to that beleaguered young clergyman in Frederick Buechner's novel. The Reverend Theodore Nicolet's self image has just been badly shaken, if not shattered, by some explosions deep within his psyche. His personal life is in something of a shambles. He can no longer hide the marks of his flawed and broken humanity even from himself, *especially* from himself. The public pose which, for the sake of ministry, he's been able to maintain in his parish has been exposed in his own eyes as being sharply different from his private reality. He sees that it isn't the pose which is sin, but the pretense that no pose is being maintained. Right in the midst of that crisis, while his whole life seems to be unravelling, we hear him sketching out loud next Sunday's sermon. It will be the Festival of Pentecost:

> *Beloved, don't believe I preach the best without knowing the worst, that's all I mean. I know it, beloved — a flop of a son, comedian of a priest. But the worst thing isn't the last thing in the world. It's the next to last thing. The last thing is the best. It's the power from on high that comes down into the world, that wells up from the rock-bottom worst of the world like a hidden spring ... the last, best thing is the laughing deep in the hearts of the saints, sometimes in our hearts even. Yes. You are terribly loved and forgiven. Yes. You are healed.*[1]

"Can a Christian also be a minister in the church?" I believe the answer to that question is never self-evident or unambiguous, any more than is the answer to any serious human question.

There is hope for us, however, as long as we keep discovering and rediscovering that we carry the treasure of the gospel not only in "earthen vessels" but in *broken* ones. Broken vessels are the kind God seems to delight most in using. God is, after all, the God of Abraham, Isaac and Jacob and all the other unsaintly saints of Israel. God is also the God of Peter and Paul and Francis and Luther and Calvin and King, all part of the long procession of those whose fractured humanity was plainly seen but graciously used.

This should not surprise us, for God is also the God of the cross and of the earthen vessel broken there for the life of the world.

---

1. Frederick Buechner. *The Final Beast* (Altheneum: New York, 1965), pp. 174-175.

Thieves

Some of the most compelling images of ministry are derived from those which the New Testament employs for Jesus and his ministry. Sometimes the image is set before us in terms of polarity. Jesus is "Lord" or "Master"; we are "servants," or in the even stronger language of Saint Paul, "slaves of Christ."

Other images are in terms of correspondence. Jesus is "the Light of the world"; but he also calls his disciples "the light of the world." They are reflected light, to be sure, as with the moon from the sun, but light nonetheless. Again, Jesus is "the Good Shepherd" and we his undershepherds, a pastoral image in which a traditional title for the ordained minister is rooted.

There is one New Testament image for Jesus and his ministry, however, which we have never hurried to borrow. Jesus employs it of himself in one of those brief parables of the Kingdom in Saint Matthew's Gospel:

> *But understand this: If the owner of the house had known at what time of night the thief was coming, he would have kept watch and would not have left his house to be broken into. So you also must be ready, because the Son of Man will come at an hour when you do not expect him. (Matthew 24:43-44).*

The image is present in an even more straightforward form in the warning the Risen Christ delivers to the drowsing church of Sardis: "... if you do not wake up, I will come like a thief, and you will not know what time I will come" (Revelation 3:36).

Jesus the Thief! There's a faint odor of blasphemy about such a notion. Yet, clearly, the earliest church wasn't nervous about using language of this kind to characterize Jesus and his work. And surely what is good enough for the Master is good enough also for his servants!

I invite you, therefore, to the odd view that the cadre of the church's leaders are called to be a pack of thieves. I find some encouragement for that perspective in a sentence in one of Flannery O'Connor's novels. She describes a God-obsessed, slightly mad preacher in her story in this way: "He proceeded about the Lord's business like an experienced crook."[1]

It's unlikely that any of us, when embarking on our journey toward ministry, saw seminary as the church's counterpart of Fagan's "school of thieves" from which we would emerge as ecclesiastical "Artful Dodgers." It is, to say the least, a peculiar lens through which to view the "holy work" in which we're engaged. Just for that reason it offers some interesting angles.

* * *

For one thing, the image of the thief suggests that a legitimate consequence of our ministries will be to relieve people of their most cherished securities.

Though I've never been robbed, I've talked to people who have. There's a terrible sense of having been violated. In spite of locks and bolts, you and your household are suddenly exposed as being vulnerable. Family jewels, treasured heirlooms, personal papers, or even less significant possessions — things which had become part of your identity — are gone! Only then do you suddenly become aware of the importance they had assumed in your life.

It's a fundamental human trait, born of our aching desire to be secure in an unstable world, that we lay up for ourselves "treasures on earth." These treasures come in innumerable forms: the achievements which undergird our egos; the possessions — material, intellectual, religious, moral — which buttress our self image; the dogmatisms behind which we attempt to establish impregnable positions; the racist or sexist biases by which we define ourselves at the expense of others. These are the familiar household gods we worship in secret, for, in Luther's words: "That upon which you set your heart and in which you place your trust is properly your god."

It was and is part of the work of Jesus and his gospel to break into these secure worlds we try to create for ourselves and despoil them. The Word which he is and of which we are servants comes as "a thief in the night." It robs us of what consciously or unconsciously we had come to count on by exposing its limited value and ultimate vulnerability. Our ministries, therefore, insofar as we are faithful, will make us his accomplices. Like it or not, we will assist him in robbing people (never excluding ourselves!) of the worth of what they may most fervently desire and of confidence in that in which they most desperately trust.

At this point, however, the metaphor falters. Real thieves rob in order to enrich themselves. Jesus is "the Good Thief," as it were, who robs in order to enrich his victims. He steals our fake jewels and cheap baubles only so that he can place in our hands "the pearl without price," which is the gospel. He reduces us to poverty so that, in our emptiness, there will be space for the immeasurable riches of grace. He strips us of false securities and illusory hopes only to establish us in the unshakable reality of a love from which nothing can separate us.

To become his skilled accomplices in *that* kind of robbery is surely worth a long apprenticeship and a continual perfecting of our skills. Jesus wills to send us out on our ministries as "Artful Dodgers" for the gospel.

* * *

This leads to a second observation suggested by the image of the thief. A "thief in the night" never barges boldly into a targeted house, slamming doors, knocking over furniture and generally making as much commotion as possible. The resourceful thief knows the value of the soft touch, looks for the most accessible means of entry and then goes in on cat's feet. I think this is what Flannery O'Connor had in mind when she said her street preacher went "about the Lord's business like an experienced crook." Some bitter lessons, which need not be recounted here, had taught him the wisdom of patience.

An experienced thief also learns to discover where it's worthwhile making a strike. Not every possible robbery justifies the effort necessary to carry it off. Likewise, not every issue which emerges in the fulfillment of our ministries is worthy of a major campaign. Some issues, to be sure, are, and to avoid them is to compromise the integrity of our calling. The universality of the gospel — its inclusiveness of all people without regard to ethnic origin, color, social rank, sexual orientation — is most certainly one such issue. Whether the paraments at Easter should be white or gold just as certainly is not. Like Flannery O'Connor's "experienced crook," the wise leader will develop a fine sense of which issues on the spectrum are worth the cost of an incursion.

For cost, it is certain, there will be. No thief can pursue his or her career without risk. People and churches, communities and nations don't like having their values questioned, their priorities challenged, their securities threatened. Thieves who persist in trying to break into such carefully ordered and closely guarded worlds are sooner or later going to get caught and pay the price.

When that happens to us in the course of our ministries, we should remember that we couldn't possibly be in better company. The line of Jesus' accomplices is a long one, stretching from Saint Paul to Luther to Bunyan to Martin Luther King, Jr. All of them served time for the sake of the gospel. The "crimes" for which they were accountable didn't pay — by the world's usual way of reckoning.

Above all, we should remember Jesus himself. He came and he comes like "a thief in the night." Finally they caught him, threw him in jail and strung him up to die. But then came the robbery to top them all. He broke into death's stronghold and robbed it of its sting. Through all the centuries since, the church has never stopped talking about it.

---

1. Flannery O'Connor. *The Violent Bear It Away* (Farrar, Straus & Cudahy: New York, 1955, 1960), p. 62.

Waiters

Sometime ago the *New York Times* carried a fascinating article about the decline and fall of the art of waiting on tables. "Top notch professional staffs have become an endangered species," moaned the author. "... the general level of performance in most restaurants could be described as casual at best."[1]

I thought about that afterward, because there are some obvious analogies between the vocation of being a waiter or waitress and our callings to lay and ordained ministries. In fact, the work of waiting on tables may be the closest contemporary equivalent for one of the primary biblical metaphors for our callings under Christ. "For which is greater," Jesus once asked the disciples, "one who sits at table or one who serves? Is it not the one who sits at table? But I am among you as one who serves" (Luke 22:27). Furthermore, they were to mirror this radical reversal of roles as they followed him: "... whoever would be great among you must be your servant, and whoever would be first among you must be slave of all" (Mark 10:43b-44).

There are deep Old Testament roots to this imagery, chief among them Isaiah's "Servant Songs." But I've always been fascinated by an unpretentious vignette which lies almost hidden in the middle of Psalm 123:

> *Behold, as the eyes of servants*
> *look to the hand of their master,*
> *as the eye of a maid*
> *to the hand of her mistress,*
> *so our eyes look to the Lord our God,*
> *till he have mercy upon us. (123:2)*

There's the very picture of a perfect servant: standing poised and ready until summoned or released by the merest gesture from mistress or master. Or, to return to the image with which we began, the Lord's servant is like a good waitress or waiter, always on the alert for the slightest hint from a table of diners that some service is required.

Many are the qualities needed by a good waiter (and, for economy's sake let's agree on the originally gender neutral noun), and surely high among them is this willingness to be at the disposal of others. Prompt and gracious service is expected of a waiter, whether the diners are considerate or cantankerous, show gratitude or take everything for granted. And personal agendas must be set aside. Service is to proceed no matter what one's preoccupations or inner climate may be on a given day.

One of our most persistent tests of ministry comes at precisely this point. Self-abnegation isn't an innately human trait. Self-protection is. Our egos clamor incessantly to have their demands met, their needs fulfilled, their rights respected. Neither ordination nor commissioning nor any other rite of the church silences that clamoring.

One pastor I know has handled this problem by keeping his telephone number unlisted. Not for him bothersome calls in the middle of the night — or, for that matter, in the middle of the day! Yet, the fact is, God's first signal that a waiter is needed often comes in the form of an interruption of our carefully planned schedules.

The place at which the ordained regularly and paradigmatically act out their role as waiters is the Table of the Lord. Our present habit of naming the officiating minister "the president of the Eucharist" tends to obscure the fact that this is the *Lord's* Table and not ours. *He* is the Host, and we, even though "presiding," are among his guests. It might be more appropriate for us to think of ourselves as the waiters at this meal, serving food and drink to the faithful as the disciples distributed the multiplied loaves and fish to the multitudes. And this table service we render the gathered people of God is a ritualized enactment of the attentive way we're to "wait on" these same guests all week long when they're scattered in the world. Eucharistic catering and pastoral care are to reflect and reinforce each other.

Of course, such "waitering" in the church is never a one-directional activity, flowing only from pastor or lay professional to people. The church is a company of waiters in which each anticipates and serves the needs of all. And together this company waits upon the needs of the world, serving the Bread of Life, which is the gospel, to those whose hunger may not be immediately apparent, speaking for those whom our society silences, refusing to forget those whom it neglects and rejects, struggling to make this planet home a banquet hall in which God's lavish gifts are equitably distributed and peaceably enjoyed. In this sense, the vocation of waiter, as defined by Jesus, is radically subversive of a society oriented toward unrestrained consumption and unlimited exercise of power. We are called to model and work for the formation of communities of waiters who will be servants of Jesus, the Head Waiter of us all.

* * *

So far I've been using the noun "waiter" and the verb form "to wait on" in their active sense. But there's also a proper way of using these words in a passive mode.

To "wait" can mean to suspend activity until something happens over which we have little, if any, control. Thus, we wait for a letter to come, the phone to ring, a friend to arrive. We may nervously drum our fingers, restlessly pace the floor, or even occassionally climb the wall, but nothing we do can hasten or achieve that for which we wait. The matter is literally out of our hands.

This is an element of ministry no less important than the active role I've described. In every aspect of our service in the church we find ourselves waiting upon responses we can't govern.

Preaching is an obvious example. Having prepared the nourishing food of the Word as carefully and imaginatively as we know how (certainly with much thought about the dietary needs of the prospective diners) and having served it appropriately in the actual event of preaching, then we must wait courteously and patiently on the outcome. We cannot force the response of our hearers. It's entirely out of *our* hands now, but thankfully in the far more trustworthy hands of the Spirit who (also without manipulation) "calls, gathers, enlightens and sanctifies" those who form the Body of Christ.

This principle holds not only in preaching but in pastoral care, teaching, social advocacy, administration and all other facets of ministry. Knowing when to back off and *wait* is as important as knowing when to get up and *do*. Fussy waiters who are always hovering over their diners and imposing themselves upon them can spoil an otherwise good meal. Indeed, some of our most productive times with the people we serve may be precisely when we appear to be doing the least. I love that apparently nonchalant farmer in Jesus' parable who, having sown the seed, goes to bed and sleeps the sleep of the just, and the seed sprouts and grows "he knows not how" (Mark 4:26-29).

W. H. Vanstone, in a remarkable book titled *The Stature Of Waiting*, interprets Jesus' passion by this image. Having done all that total, active love could possibly do, Jesus allows himself to be handed over to his enemies and awaits their verdict on his ministry. Jesus, who has been endlessly active on behalf of others, waiting on their needs "hand and foot," as we say, is now by his own choice reduced to passive waiting upon others. He makes himself vulnerable to their response and finally helpless before their wrath.

Yet it's in the moment of absolute waiting, when on the cross all possibility of initiative is taken away from him, that the power of God is most compellingly manifest: ". . . and I," Jesus says, "when I am lifted up (note the passive form!) from the earth, will draw all people to myself" (John 12:32).

Our calling, then, is to be shaped by this Lord who took upon himself the role of a waiter. Whether we take that term in either its active or passive sense, Jesus is its paradigm. He made himself totally available to the world in that "waiting upon" which is the service of love. He made himself wholly vulnerable to the world in that "waiting upon" which is another name for prayer. We need the molding power of the Spirit to shape our ministries in both modes and to help us discern when each is required.

---

1. Bryan Miller. *New York Times,* September 4, 1985, Section C, p. 1.

Stars

One Christmas I received from one of my sons a large and fascinating book. It was a richly textured study of a tiny village in Nothern Ireland named Balleymenone. No aspect of its life was left untouched — its work and leisure, its land and houses, its people and their songs and stories. Most impressive to me was a small group of men, three or four at the most, who were known within the community as "stars." They were the singers of its songs and the tellers of its tales. No one had appointed them to this role. They had no official status, no "ordination papers," so to speak. They were simply recognized as "stars" by virtue of their gifts and the disciplined and generous way they spent those gifts in the service of the community.

Analogously, we are the "stars' within those Christian communities we serve. Clearly there are hazards in such an image. Taken in one way it can only encourage certain unfortunate tendencies in our egos which generally don't require much encouragement. In spite of such dangers, the image is worth examining.

As indicated, the stars of Balleymenone are the singers of the community's songs and the tellers of its tales. They lay no claim to original and creative genius. They are not the composers of their material but receive it from a tradition which links them with ancestors stretching back beyond memory. Generation after generation, stars have passed on stories of saints and heroes, of bandits and battles. The current stars feel a responsibility for the preservation of that tradition and, beyond that, for its interpretation. What they receive dare not be lost, but it may be — indeed *must* be — altered, embellished, rearranged, retold in such a way that facts transcend themselves in truth and the distant past interprets the emergent present.

* * *

Once during a symposium on international relations I heard a political scientist (who had earlier introduced himself as a "story teller") describe our present world crisis in this way: "We are all in trouble, because we are between stories. The old story is gone, and we don't have a new story to tell."
He was correct, of course, insofar as he was talking about the dismal story we human beings have been telling one another, with only superficial variations, for aeons. It's the story of our quest for security through the accumulation of wealth and power; the story of our drive to dominate our neighbors and those dependent upon us for what it sometimes pleases us to call "their own good"; the story of our wresting from the earth her ancient secrets and turning them to destruction; the story of our seizing the Creator's wondrous gifts as though they were ours to possess; the story of our endless sacrifices to the gods Moloch, Mammom and Machine. That story *is*, in fact, dead and gone, or, put better, it has brought us, with all our sisters and brothers in the human family, to the brink of death. And we possess neither the wisdom to create nor the eloquence to relate a new story which leads to life.

But the church into whose service we're called knows a secret. It knows by faith that we are not "between stories" at all. We are *within* a story. We live in the flow of the plot of *the* Story, a story as old as "the Ancient of Days" and as new as tomorrow's dawn. It begins, "in the beginning," when God blew his winds over the void and breathed his breath into a lump of clay. It tells of a fall and an expulsion from a garden and of a relentless but loving pursuit of humanity in its flight. It tells of the calling of a people who will sing the songs of the chosen and speak of judgment and mercy to the nations. It tells, at its center, of a life and a death and a resurrection. It drives on and still drives on toward its ending in a new heaven and a new earth whose promise is beyond humanity's brightest dreams.

It is of this matchless story that we have been named the tellers. We have been set like stars in the darkness of a generation that has lost hope because it has forgotten the story.

How to tell it with accuracy and interpret it with authenticity is the chief burden of our special calling.

Earlier I noted that there is a certain peril in this imagery of the star. In a society without saints, we have energetically manufactured stars — rock stars, media stars, sports stars. Star cults are a form of natural religion in a secular culture. And, like most minor deities, stars delight in the adoration of their worshippers and profit greatly from their offerings.

The same danger is present in our ministries. In a church too infected by its culture and led by us humans, vulnerable to pride, star cults are easily born. Ministerial fantasies can lead us perilously close to that dream of the youthful Joseph who set his brothers' teeth on edge: "Behold, I have dreamed another dream; and behold the sun, the moon, and eleven stars were bowing down to me" (Genesis 37:9). The willingness of people to offer adulation and our readiness to receive it is a heady and hazardous mixture from which we daily need deliverance.

In Balleymenone there is a saying: "Stars must not make themselves look bright." Kierkegaard was pointing to something like that when he described the difference between a genius and an apostle. A genius is brilliant, shining in and for his or her own glory. An apostle is faithful, called only to reflect the glory of another.

It will help us in our ministries if we remember that the Light of that Other whose glory we are to reflect shone brightest when eclipsed by pain and death. Only when his Light was extinguished and "darkness covered the whole earth" did his Father rekindle it to blaze forth in its fullness. Stars shine as they are consumed — whether Jesus, "the bright and morning Star," forever risen and never going down, or ourselves who are called to shine, however faintly, with his reflected light.

Poets

John Henry Newman, leader of the nineteenth century Oxford Movement and later a convert to Roman Catholicism, was also an innovative educator. He once defined the nature of education in this manner: "True education consists in unlearning life's poetry and learning its prose."

My first reaction to that sentence was to fight with it. If those engaged in education did manage to bleach the poetry out of students' souls, it would be nothing short of pedagogical crime. "Life's poetry," I would argue is a dimension of existence to which we are usually far too blind. Our perceptions of it, therefore, need to be sharpened rather than dulled.

There is even a sense, as John Donne reminds us, in which God may be described as a poet. He writes in one of his sermons:

> *Read the Bible and you will see that ours is a figurative, a metaphoricall God ...; a God in whose words there is such a flight of figures, such voyages, such peregrinations to fetch remote and previous metaphors ... as all prophane Authors seeme of the seede of the Serpent that crepes," (whereas the scriptures are as) "the dove that flies.*[1]

The Psalmist even affirms that there is an aspect of beauty in the very holiness of God. God's goodness and power are altogether grace-full. God's handiwork in creation is more than strictly utilitarian. Nature doesn't just "work." Earth and sky are crammed with delights beyond describing. And when, "in the fullness of time," God entered history in a radically new way, he didn't hurl himself at creation with all the finesse of a neighborhood bully. God came in "grace" as well as "truth." And grace has in its composition an element of beauty.

It's significant that the Greek adjective *kalos* used by John when he calls Jesus "the Good Shepherd" can be translated either good or beautiful. John is clearly denoting something more in Jesus than a kind of right-angled morality. He's pointing to a quality which was righteous without being repellent, holy and yet winsome.

To be sure, there were those who found Jesus such an offense that they hounded him to his death. But the evangelists don't fail to note another side of the response of his contemporaries: "Everyone is looking for you!" the disciples tell him excitedly early one morning (Mark 1:37). Or again, "The common people heard him gladly" (Mark 12:37). Many were drawn to this beautifully good shepherd as by a magnet — a magnet of grace made powerful by total and costly self-giving. What other explanation is there for the motley assortment of sheep he gathered — and still gathers — around himself?

So, Cardinal Newman to the contrary notwithstanding, I would insist that the goal of education before and after our entrance into ministry is *not* to "unlearn life's poetry," at least insofar as that poetry reflects the poetry and grace of the gospel. Rather, it's important that the cadence and style of our ministries be permanently conditioned by the rhyme and rhythm of grace. Certainly the inevitable and necessary scandal of the gospel shouldn't bear the additional burden of ministerial lives that disfigure its grace. To put it in the more positive words of Titus, we're to "adorn (literally, 'decorate,' 'garnish') the doctrine of God our Savior" by our life and conversation (2:20).

I suspect that Newman, who was himself a poet of some gifts, wouldn't quarrel with any of this. He really intended something else by his dictum. Far from rejecting the gifts of grace and beauty which the gospel embodies, he meant his words to be an antidote to an unhealthy romanticism which can easily grip us and limit our effectiveness as servants of the Word. It's in this sense that we're to unlearn life's poetry and learn its prose.

Newman is surely accurate in his perception that life does indeed have substantial quantities of prose to be mastered. Marriage is a familiar example. We enter it sufficiently starry-eyed that there is little chance of our seeing far down the road to be travelled. Love may not be blind, but it's certainly nearsighted. Then come the years of burnt toast and bruised feelings, of dishes in the sink and diapers that stink, of chores that never end and ends that never meet. Often it isn't the big crises on which marriages shipwreck but simply the incapacity to cope with the prosaic, to come to grips with the fact, as a church father wrote, that we "may not be taken up and transported to our journey's end, but must travel thither on foot, traversing the whole distance of the narrow way." In Peter DeVries' exceedingly unromantic, unpoetic definition: "A good marriage is sticking with what you're stuck with."

Most of us would want to say a good deal more than that about our marriages and, by analogy about our ministries. Yet DeVries' words have a proper application to both. A disproportionate amount of what we do in fulfilling our vocations often seems more like prose we're "stuck with" than poetry to be set to music: completing bothersome reports for ecclesiastical bureaucracies, keeping tedious parish records, making calls we don't feel like making, doing sermon preparation which some weeks feels like plodding through mud, persisting in the basic tasks of our office when there are no results that can be plotted on a graph. In the end, the true value of our ministry may have more to do with how we handle tedium and obscurity — the prose of our callings — than how we celebrate the occasional flashes of poetry along the way.

Once while waiting between services at a supply appointment in an old Pennsylvania congregation, I passed the time by browsing through a copy of its history. There, sandwiched between accounts of the notable achievements of some of its early pastors, was this crushing one-liner about a poor fellow whose name I don't even remember: "Nothing of note happened during his ministry."

"What?" I almost shouted. Were there no babies baptized, no children catechized and confirmed, no sick visited, no dead committed to their Maker, no sermons preached, no Lord's Suppers administered, no day in and day out care of the flock which the Holy Spirit had placed in this pastor's charge? "Nothing of note happened . . . ?" Are only the novel, the dramatic, the publicizable — those accomplishments which merit a paragraph in a congregational history — worth remembering and celebrating?

I sincerely hope not, for in ministry, as in all of life, the prose is more plentiful than the poetry, and Newman is right in insisting that we learn how to deal with it. Otherwise we will "stand (most) of the day idle" and merit our Lord's hard judgment of that worthless servant who buried his one poor, prosaic talent in the earth.

But I would also argue that prose, touched by grace, becomes its own kind of poetry. Those who are faithful over little enter daily into the deeper joy of their Lord. The Light of the world illumines those obscure corners in which they serve. Even the most routine task becomes a word, a syllable, a letter which contributes to the rhyme and rhythm of the gospel.

It may be that James had something like this in mind when he exhorted his readers: "Be doers (the Greek noun is *poietai*) . . . be *poets* of the word . . . ." And that we can become through the quickening power of the One who translated even the prose of death into the poetry of life.

---

1. Quoted in William R. Mueller. *John Donne: Preacher* (Princeton University Press: Princeton, 1962), p. 30.

Spies

Some years ago, while reading a commentary whose author and title I can no longer remember, I ran across an ancient writer's characterization of the sage or wise man as a "spy of God" in the world. The commentator was using that metaphor to interpret the ministry of Jesus and his disciples. By extension, it's a suggestive lens through which to look at our ministries.

Spies of God! On the surface, that phrase may seem to have little to commend it for ministry in the church. Spies must often operate by principles that range from the questionable to the despicable. As we meet them in film and fiction, their methods include deceit, bribery, seduction, theft and murder. Not exactly the basis for a code of professional ethics! Yet there are characteristics of a spy's life and work that are intriguing.

* * *

For example, spies have an understandable reluctance to call attention to themselves.

A few years ago John LeCarre gave a fictional portrait of *A Perfect Spy*. When we first meet Magnus Pym, he's living in a shabby room in a run-down boarding house in a rather seedy English seaside town. He's the most ordinary looking man imaginable. You could easily mistake him for the village butcher. Actually he's passing himself off as a minor civil servant on vacation. Nobody could ever guess that he's one of Britain's top international spies.

That isn't a bad role model for those of us whose vocation it is to keep calling attention to Another rather than to ourselves. We aren't so much "little Christs" in our ministries as we are "little John the Baptists" whose function must always be to point away from ourselves toward "the Lamb of

God who takes away the sin of the world." "He must increase, but (we) must decrease" (John 3:30).

The prominent and central positions we're called to occupy in the midst of God's people makes it easy for us to forget that. Lines of attention in the parish, all week long but especially on Sunday morning, run straight toward ourselves. That's an awesome fact but also a heady one, making it tempting for us to think of ourselves more highly than we ought to think.

Kierkegaard's famous parable of the theater is a good antidote for our susceptibility to this disease. On Sunday morning, he says, most Christians think of the church as a theater in which the pastor has the lead role, declaiming from center stage, with the people as the passive, listening audience out there in front. Not so, Kierkegaard insists! The church is a theater in which *God* is the Listener, the people are the actors and preachers are the prompters.

Not a very glamorous role! But, as with a good prompter or "a perfect spy," faithfulness in ministry counts for more than flash, self-abnegation more than self-aggrandizement.

* * *

Consider also the fact that most spies spend a major part of their working lives in a country not their own. They're aliens in a foreign land, always to some degree strangers among the people to whom they're sent.

There are clear biblical undertones in such a statement. "Go from your country and your father's house," God commands Abraham, "to that land that I will show you" (Genesis 12:1). "I have been a stranger in a foreign land," says Moses by way of introduction to Jethro, his prospective father-in-law (Exodus 2:22). "Our citizenship is in heaven," writes Saint Paul to the members of the congregation in Philippi (Philippians 3:20).

Many of us, when we leave seminary, look forward to "settling in" after the discontinuities of our seminary years. We're ready to put down roots, furnish a house, plant a garden, establish solid relationships in a stable community. There's a positive side to this human yearning for something more than transiency. It may incline us to remain in our places of ministry long enough to make a difference.

But there's a reverse side also. "Here we have no continuing city," is the Word of the Lord to us (Hebrews 13:14). The call of God has a way of unsettling and uprooting us, keeping us from ever becoming too settled in whatever land it is to which we go. This will be true even if we remain in the same parish for a lifetime. The Word of the Lord will sometimes be a word that alienates us from the very people to whom we're most deeply attached. It will keep us from ever becoming completely at home, even in the best of parishes in the best of times. Without seeking martyrdom or cultivating conflict, the Word of the Lord will, on occasion, force us against all our inclinations to be, like Jeremiah, "a fortified city, an iron pillar, and bronze walls, against the whole land in which (we) serve" (Jeremiah 1:18). That's the inescapable loneliness of the servant of the Word, the "spy of God."

Related to this incapacity ever fully to settle in and be at home — related as both cause and consequence — is another characteristic of a spy: A good spy develops a keen nose for truth.

A major part of a spy's role in a foreign land is to sniff out the difference between illusion and reality. What's actually going on behind the scenes? What facts about this country — its political currents, its military preparedness, its economic condition — lie hidden beneath the surface of its life? A spy operates with what is called in some theological circles a healthy "hermeneutic of suspicion."

Obviously I'm not suggesting that one of our highest joys in ministry should be that of spying out the faults and failings of the people among whom we serve. I can think of no more repulsive a figure than a moral snoop.

And yet there's something about the Word of God which necessarily separates truth from falsehood, reality from illusion. Under its laser beam "there's nothing covered up that will not be made known" (Luke 12:2). I suppose a top spy develops a gift for that kind of penetrating discernment — the capacity to see below the surface of things and events, to read clues to reality that escape the rest of us.

And it's a gift of the Spirit for which "the spy of God" must pray. We live and serve in a society and culture saturated with illusion. Only consider the billions spent annually on advertising in an effort to convince us that life with a capital "L" is only possible if we own this particular car, or dress in that particular fashion, or indulge in this particular pleasure, or accumulate these particular securities.

How hard it is for any of us, enmeshed as we all are in our society's network of power and privilege, to see through such illusions to the realities of oppression and disadvantage they lay upon persons of another race or gender or nation! The "spy of God," like her or his secular counterpart, will develop a sure sense for the delusions and distortions by which truth is veiled in our culture, allowing the Word of God to expose them for what they are.

But here the analogy, like all analogies, begins to falter. We're agents of a kingdom whose truth is inseparable from grace. We serve a king who came among us not to condemn but to give life. Our spying, like that of Jesus, the one "perfect Spy," isn't in the interest of dominance or oppression but of service and liberation. We announce a Word able to bring persons that fullness of life they seek elsewhere. We proclaim a Word whose power will finally break the bonds of all oppressors and give the poor and afflicted their inheritance.

* * *

You will recall that deep in the pages of the Old Testament there's a marvellous spy story. Moses and his band of runaway slaves have just reached the borders of the land of promise, and Moses sends representatives of the 12 tribes "to spy out the land of Canaan." Ten of them come back panting for the "milk and honey" they found there but terrified by the apparent military superiority of the Canaanites. They bring Moses a counsel of despair: He should sound retreat! But Caleb and

Joshua offer a minority report: "Let us go up at once and occupy (the land); for we are well able to overcome it" (Numbers 13:30).

It's with that assurance that we "spy out the land" to which God sends us in our ministries. We go in the service of a kingdom whose resources are unlimited and of a king whose grace is inexhaustible.

Nightwatchers

One of the occupations I've watched fade into almost total oblivion during my lifetime is that of the nightwatchman. In the northern Pennsylvania town where I grew up, every factory had one. All night long they occupied tiny offices in dark, silent buildings, occasionally making rounds of the premises for whose security they were responsible. While the rest of us slept in our beds, there they were, lonely sentries at their posts. In a small town like ours they fought boredom more than fear.

Today watchmen, like blacksmiths and shoemakers, are an endangered species. Their unromantic replacements are guard dogs and electronic surveillance systems. The one exception is in the church. Each spring the church certifies a whole new cadre of nightwatchmen and nightwatchwomen to stand duty in thousands of congregations across the land. They join the ranks of those whom a Psalmist describes as the "servants of the Lord (who) stand by night in the house of the Lord" (Psalm 134:1).

* * *

Like those sentinels of my childhood, the church's nightwatchers are, to state the obvious, responsible for something. It's been popular in recent years to refer to those who fill roles of public ministry in the church as "guardians of the gospel." That phrase has always struck me as odd, even wrong-headed. It seems closer to the truth to say that the gospel guards the church, not we the gospel. The safety of the gospel, thank God, is ultimately in God's hands, not ours.

Nevertheless, the phrase "guardians of the gospel" points to something that's true. The message of God's free and unconditional love poured out upon us in the life, death and resurrection of Jesus *does* need defense against human tendencies to compromise or undermine it. Certainly in the world, but also in the church, there are always those ready to preach another gospel — a "non-gospel" or an "anti-gospel" — which adulterates both God's unconditional gift of love and God's absolute demand for faithfulness. There's a perverse twist in our human nature which is forever turning the message of free grace into non-grace, on the one hand, or into "cheap grace," on the other. And those called to public ministries in the church are to be, in Saint Paul's words, "stewards of the mysteries of God," — "guardians of the gospel," who will stand watch by day and by night over its integrity against all who threaten it.

* * *

But there's another sense in which ministry is nightwatch. Those who envision their vocation as being primarily a bright daytime operation are headed for disillusion. Ministry is full of night duty.

Sometimes that's literally true. A call comes at 2 a.m. that a parishioner has met a tragic death, and the family needs us. We go to bed tormented by a crisis in the parish or burdened with the knowledge of our own foolishness or failure, and we twist and turn until dawn. There are times when the weight of ministry makes sleep a stranger and night seem endless.

As we all know, there's a kind of night that has nothing to do with the hour hand on the clock. It's the kind of night a Psalmist was talking about when he prayed, "O my God, I cry in the *daytime*, but you do not answer" (Psalm 22:2a).

He knew, as we know, the demons of doubt, guilt, pride and fear which lurk round the clock in the shadows of our souls. Sometimes we can find no words of prayer or assurances of scripture to slay them. We who speak the Word of Promise to others may hear for ourselves only the terrible silence of the absence of God.

Nothing can shelter us from this darkness. We may live in the bosom of a loving family and be surrounded by caring people, yet again and again life and ministry will bring us to what Kierkegaard called "the midnight hour when we must unmask" and confront in ourselves the alienation and brokenness that make us one with the people who look to us for ministry.

We're never excused from that nightwatch. We can only remember, when we stand there, that our lonely vigil is shared by One upon whom earth's deepest darkness descended and who yet cried to God out of God-forsakenness. It is often only in retrospect that we can confess with Saint Augustine: "... it is only at night that he declares his pity."[1]

* * *

Many times, however, as suggested above, the night duty we stand will be on behalf of others — perhaps that actual 2 a.m. ring of the phone that summons us to descend with another human being into a darkness of spirit or circumstance we'd like nothing better than to evade.

Camus, in his novel *The Fall*, tells of a prisoner of war who challenges the indifferent universe, which seems utterly oblivious to his fate, with the question, "Who will sleep on the floor for us?"[2]

We, of course, proclaim the gospel of the Incarnation as the ultimate response to that question. It is God who came "to sleep on the floor for us" in the stable in Bethlehem. But the question is also an unspoken one our people will often be asking of us, as witnesses to the Incarnation: "Who will sleep on the floor with *us*?" Is there anyone to enter with us into our darkness?

Everything in our humanity will often be inclined to draw back from that question but, if we're faithful, we'll nonetheless go. And there, in the nightwatch of pastoral care, we discover a grace that transcends our fear and self-doubt and shines into the darkness a light from beyond us.

* * *

Finally, let it be said that only those who stand nightwatch are in position to announce the dawn.

Think back to those thousands of monks and nuns cloistered away in monasteries and convents scattered across the forests and plains of Europe during the period we call the Dark Ages. The lamps of learning and of faith were in danger of being extinguished by the hordes of barbarians sweeping across Christendom. But all through that night the candles which flickered in remote chapels signalled the presence of a light "no darkness could overcome." As the Psalmist sang, "Blessed are those who stand by night in the house of the Lord ..."; and he might have added, "for it is they who will at last announce the dawn."

Of course, our situation is radically different. We live in a society which is tempted to believe it has already overcome the darkness. Through the technology of illumination, we're literally able to make the night shine as the day. The danger is that the astonishing human achievements of this twentieth century will persuade us that earth's morning has come and there's no more darkness to fear.

One of our roles as nightwatchers will be to announce to the "secular city" that it's 2 a.m. and all is *not* well: that the securities, personal and national, with which we surround ourselves; the comforts and pleasures we have at our fingertips; the scientific advances of which we're so proud — all of this is *artificial* light which only *seems* to overcome the darkness in ourselves and in our world.

But, in the end, our chief purpose isn't to "tell of the night" but to announce the dawn. We're called to be heralds of the advent into this darkling world of Him who came as "Light from Light," who on Easter morning shone more brightly than the sun and who, at last, will triumph over all earth's darkness.

* * *

Listen now to another Psalmist's words about our vocation as nightwatchers: "Unless the Lord watches over the city, in vain the (watchers) keep vigil" (Psalm 127:2).

His point isn't to denigrate the importance of those human sentinels, like ourselves, who keep vigil for and with the people of God. No, his point is to reassure us! Because God does everlastingly stand watch over "the City of God," we who also watch can watch in hope. The God who calls us to night duty is the Lord God of Israel who "neither slumbers nor sleeps."

That's why those who "stand by night in the house of the Lord" are able to announce the dawn.

It's the burden and the glory of our calling.

---

1. St. Augustine. *The Nicene And Post-Nicene Fathers* (Wm. B. Eerdmans: Grand Rapids, 1989), Vol. VII, p. 136.

2. Albert Camus. *The Fall* (Alfred A. Knopf, Inc.: New York, 1956), p. 32.

Fools

Bernard of Clairvaux wrote in one of his letters: "Play the mountebank I will .... A good sort of playing which is ridiculous to men, but a very beautiful sight to the angels."[1]

He is not alone in viewing the ministry of God's servants through the image of the fool. Saint Paul said of himself and his fellow missionaries: "We are fools for Christ's sake, while you are such sensible Christians" (1 Corinthians 4:10). One of Saint Francis' biographers has written that when the saint "came forth from his cave of vision, he was wearing the ... word 'fool' as a feather in his cap. He would go on being a fool; he would become more and more of a fool; he would be the court fool of the King of Paradise."[2] And, as a recent study of Luther reminds us, the reformer once described himself as "God's court jester."[3]

* * *

In the eyes of many, the very decision to enter some form of ministry in the church wins us that label. By our choice we've already "made fools of ourselves." No longer is the "parson" or the lay professional the chief personage of a community, universally admired, automatically looked up to, listened to with rapt and unquestioning attention. It would be fruitless to argue that in the late twentieth century the church's ministry enjoys status or authority remotely comparable to that of a fourteenth century priest or a seventeenth century Puritan divine. Centers of power and influence have shifted elsewhere in our society.

At one level, we've made what many would evaluate to be an economically foolish vocational choice. In spite of more generous compensation packages and better pension plans, the church's servants are unlikely to find themselves in the highest tax brackets. Potential affluence is one of the bridges we willingly burn behind us, and there are many, perhaps within our own families, who count us foolish to have done so.

Though, unlike Saint Francis, we may take no vows of poverty, nevertheless, commitment to values that have nothing to do with accumulation, can make us signs of a different kingdom. There *are* higher goods in this world than wealth, security, luxury, pleasure. While no Christian disdains the good things of God's creation, we take seriously Jesus' Word that life doesn't consist of the abundance of what we possess. The fool, writes a spiritual guide of the Eastern church, "lives life in reverse." The fool dares to say that the emperors who strut through the world flaunting other values are, in reality, wearing no clothes.

Our call to ministries of the gospel joins us with God's company of fools who dare to make "Safety Last" their motto rather than "Safety First." Insofar as we are able to follow, even at a distance, him who "had no place to lay his head," we become signs that contradict the wisdom of the world with the supreme folly of the cross.

* * *

Consider also the nature of the ministries in which we serve. They are such that we will often view other professionals in our communities as being much more efficient and effective.

How I sometimes envied those confident looking white-coated physicians I encountered while making hospital rounds! They probably didn't feel all the confidence for which I gave them credit, but they ministered to my members with a whole arsenal of drugs and technologies and could track their daily progress on a chart at the foot of the bed. All I had to offer were insubstantial words and a crumb of bread and a sip of wine whose efficacy it was impossible to measure.

And how strange what goes on in the average church on an average Sunday morning must appear to somebody on the outside! A woman or man in odd clothing stands up in a box in an often undistinguished room and speaks words which she or he knows have been insufficiently prepared and are now being inadequately communicated. Out in front, lined in rows, is a motley group of people, in which gray is often the predominant hair color, with here and there a wailing baby or a pair of whispering adolescents. They may be looking us straight in the eye, but chances are their minds are stuck on last night's family quarrel or this afternoon's trip to the mountains. No wonder Saint Paul exclaims that "... it has pleased God through the *foolishness* of preaching to save them that believe" (1 Corinthians 1:21b).

Then what follows in the service is scarcely an improvement. Those present file up to a table and eat a crumb of bread and swallow a sip of wine. Is this really "where the action is" — where what's important and significant in our world takes place? The answers, even from Christians, to any poll on that question would likely run to board rooms and power plants, research labs and command centers, not to the places where we spend most of the Sunday mornings of our lives. But then, as Saint Bernard long ago observed, God has called us to "play the fool," to do what "is ridiculous in the eyes of men, but very beautiful to the angels."

* * *

The applause of angels is reassuring to us only because our vocations force us to spend a good bit of our time learning and relearning something about *God's* foolishness. It's because God has chosen to behave that way that we are called to be fools. What a ridiculous God, from the world's perspective, God is! When God decides to challenge the pomp and power of kings and empires, God comes as a baby in a cow stall! And when God makes the decisive move to establish the authority of another kingdom, it's through a man dying on a cross!

It would be difficult to disagree with one writer's assessment of Jesus as "the greatest fool in history." Jesus demonstrated that dramatically when he led the triumphal procession into his nation's capital ... on the back of a donkey! Was he deliberately "playing the fool" that day — mocking every military parade that ever was or will be? Was he holding up to ridicule a world that is always trying to convince itself that horses and chariots, tanks and missiles are more powerful than truth and holiness and love?

And God continues to "stoop to folly" in history's ongoing drama. The church in whose ministries we serve is generally without visible power in the nerve centers of the world's life. The church often looks like a "ship of fools" when it steers against the tides of injustice and self-indulgence that run so powerfully in our society.

Likewise, as God's servants, we may not be among those whom IBM or the CIA would place at the top of their recruiting lists. God doesn't put a premium on mediocrity or incompetence, but neither does God disdain those whose gifts are not what the world might define as "the right stuff," but who willingly offer themselves to be fools for the sake of the gospel.

Yet, as we go out on our "fools' errands," we are heartened by the remembrance that we serve a God whose "foolishness is wiser than human wisdom, and (whose) weakness is stronger than human strength" (1 Corinthians 1:25). It's ultimately *God's* foolishness we're about, the foolishness of the gospel itself. We're the servants of one whose folly confounded the world's wisdom, whose weakness triumphed over all other powers, and who promises us: "My grace is sufficient for you, for my power is made perfect in weakness" (2 Corinthians 12:8).

---

1. St. Bernard of Clairvaux. *The Letters Of St. Bernard Of Clairvaux,* tr. B.S. James (Burns Oaks: London, 1953), p. 135.

2. G. K. Chesterton. *St. Francis Of Assisi* (Doubleday & Co., Inc.: New York, 1924), p. 74.

3. Eric Gritsch. *Martin — God's Court Jester* (Fortress Press: Philadelphia, 1983).

Survivors

Several years ago I participated in a retreat for clergy with a most peculiar theme: "How to Survive in the Ministry and Enjoy It." Aside from the question of whether "enjoy" is an appropriate word to attach to any consideration of the ministry of the cross, the verb "survive" is what gave me pause. It seemed to establish a rather minimal goal for the tenure of our ministry. Surely we ought to do better than merely survive!

Yet there are days when survival seems like a major victory, and, with the "drop-out" and "stop-out" rates as high as they are, just surviving in our vocations may be no mean accomplishment. What skills do we need when we leave the "boot camp" of seminary for what could be 40 or more years "at the front?" Or, to shift from a military analogy, what supplies and equipment should be in our packs for the long trek and the steep ascents ahead?

Obviously it isn't as simple as that. Our preparation for our ministries isn't an ecclesiastical version of six weeks at Fort Benning or a day's shopping at L.L.Bean. What will serve us best in the stress and conflict inevitable in ministry can't be reduced to instructions in a manual or items on a shopping list. Instead of talking about "survival tactics" or "survival equipment," I'd like to mention two perspectives that can help keep us at what Luther called the "stations" God has assigned us.

* * *

The first is *a healthy awareness that God has called us not to be successful but faithful.*

There's certainly nothing new or original about such a statement. Saint Paul meant something like that when he wrote about ministry, "... it is required of stewards that they be found trustworthy" (1 Corinthians 4:5). We all know it in our heads and repeat it with our lips, but, a good bit of the time, we live as though we don't really believe it in our hearts. The whole, prevailing drift of our achievement oriented culture conditions us to the contrary.

I'm convinced that one of the root causes of "burn out" among those in public ministries is our endemic tendency to expect more highly of ourselves than we ought to expect. There's a sad irony in the fact that we who teach and preach "justification by grace through faith" and not by works are intent upon proving our worth before God, others and, not least, ourselves, by the perfection — or at least the effectiveness — of our own work. It's an affront to our self-esteem to meet situations in which how we should minister is altogether unclear and utterly beyond our capability.

The novels of Charles Williams are strange stories in which the commonplace and the supernatural are forever and unexpectedly intersecting. The world of the Spirit intrudes without warning into events and relationships which are as ordinary as a well-worn shoe. Two central characters in one of his novels are a normally self-centered young Englishwoman and her more-than-normally pompous father. Under the mysterious pressures of grace, they're brought to a fresh and more compassionate discovery of each other. The daughter recognizes herself as "a blundering servant of Love to this other blundering servant of Love."[1]

That strikes me as a good self-image to carry with us in our ministries — not a dazzling or heroic one, but one that is healthily realistic and thoroughly biblical. It recognizes the sober fact that we usually don't stride through our tasks carrying everything before us. A good bit of the time we plod through them and often enough muddle through them, "blundering servants of Love."

This is not to make a virtue of slovenliness or a fetish of failure. In the words of the motto of George Frederick Watts, a nineteenth century painter, we're called to give "The Utmost for the Highest." Nevertheless, it is to acknowledge that incompleteness, unclarity and apparent defeat are marks by which servants of the Crucified One will be known. Such a perspective can preserve us from unseemly pride when things are going well and from unnecessary despair when they go badly, and thus increase our chances of survival.

* * *

The second perspective that can help us is *a healthy awareness that it's as blessed (and at least as difficult!) to receive as to give.*

I recognize that's the reverse of the biblical beatitude, but not, I believe, its contradiction. Indeed, a faithful hermeneutic might demand that we put it just that way in interpreting it for our situations in ministry.

Another contributing factor to "burn out" in ministry, as well as in other "serving professions," is sheer exhaustion — the conscientious effort to respond to the unremitting demand to give. There are no 40-hour weeks for those who prepare sermons, teach classes, plan worship, lead meetings, launch programs, support causes, make calls, help persons, meet crises, deal with conflicts — the list is endless. Those whose service is in the church soon learn a new and existential definition for the term "energy crisis." "Empty" isn't a designation only for fuel tanks but for depleted bodies and spirits. Nothing is more essential to survival in our callings than learning how to receive as well as give, to ingest as well as expend, to be receptors of "the means of grace" as well as their ministers.

Providentially, those "means" are always at hand for us. And they are at hand precisely in our tasks of ministry, inseparable from the very responsibilities and relationships that fill our days. It's as though right here in our normal work, God has provided one more evidence of the truth of Saint Augustine's dictum: "What God demands, God gives."

The context of our ministry is that utterly unique network of relationships which is life within "the communion of saints." More quickly than we like, we learn to use such unflattering adjectives as "petty," "stubborn," or "narrow" for specific "saints" among whom God places us to serve. Not for very long are we permitted to question the doctrine of original sin or to ignore the fact that the church in history consists of "redeemed *sinners*," always, of course, remembering to include ourselves in the formula.

But, if we are open to it, we also discover the enormous ministering power of the church of God. Ministry isn't the monopoly of the one or so of us who serve professionally within a Christian congregation. The people are, with us, "blundering servants of Love," ministers of God on our behalf, as well as we on theirs. Only when we hide our human vulnerability behind the mask of our roles do we fail to discover that "the priesthood of all the believers" is a sustaining reality as well as a theological truth.

The "means of grace" are also present for us in the particular functions of our ministries. Preparation to teach and preach, for example, can move beyond "professional task" to the level of personal engagement with the Word that has power to kill and make alive. Not only is the Word *pro istis*, "for them," the people; it is *pro nobis*, "for us" who teach and preach. The only advantage we may have over the laity we serve is the fact that we're driven by the necessity of our work to such weekly engagement with the Word of God.

Likewise, leadership of liturgy is more than "professional task," though it is certainly that. In the liturgy we not only give priestly utterance to the people's prayers; we are also surrounded and sustained by their prayer. We articulate that by the brief exchange of benediction which recurs in each liturgy: "The Lord be with you. And also with you." And at the Table we not only "preside" on behalf of Him who is the great Host of our common meal; we too are guests whose urgent hunger is duly fed. The Bread and Wine are food for *our* pilgrimage, manna to nourish us in *our* wilderness.

This leads me to say again that "survival" is too minimal a category to apply to those whose special calling is to be "servants of the servant people of God." "Survival" doesn't touch the depths of truth about our situation. It places inordinate stress upon our own qualities of dogged endurance — like that required of climbers who, lost for days in the mountains, stagger back to base more dead than alive. Ministry sometimes does require the grim determination just to "hang in," but, if that were all, the prospect would be bleak indeed.

"Deliverance" is, in my mind, a more apt and accurate rubric for our ministries. We survive, finally, only because there's One who, in the course of our life and work, intercepts us with grace that is as surprising as it is indefatigable, rescuing us even from the consequences of our own foolishness and faithlessness.

We may indeed be "blundering servants of Love," but the Love we serve and which serves us is no lower-case love. In Dante's words, it's "the Love that moves the Sun and the other stars."[2] It's also the Love that was born of Mary, nailed to a tree, raised from the tomb and now surrounds and sustains us with all its severity and tenderness.

---

1. Charles Williams.

2. Dante Alighieri. *The Divine Comedy,* tr. John Ciardi (W.W. Norton & Co.: New York, 1954), p. 601.

Sowers

"Listen! A sower went out to sow. And it happened that as he sowed, some seed fell along the footpath; and the birds came and ate it up. Some seed fell on rocky ground where it had no depth of earth; but when the sun rose the young corn was scorched, and as it had no root it withered away. Some seed fell among thistles; and the thistles shot up and choked the corn, and it yielded no crop. And some of the seed fell into good soil, where it came up and grew, and bore fruit; and the yield was thirtyfold, sixtyfold, even a hundredfold." He added, "If you have ears to hear, then hear." (Mark 4:3-9 — NEB)

Listening to Jesus' parables is like walking down a hall of mirrors. At every step, you meet yourself. So it is in this familiar parable. And the most natural place for those of us in public ministry to catch our reflection is in the figure of the sower.

My own image of the sower has been permanently conditioned by a large bas-relief on the wall facing the entrance of the old Biblical Seminary in New York City. In this artist's conception, the sower is a giant of a man — more Paul Bunyan than Johnny Appleseed. Dressed in knee-length burlap, biceps bulging, bag slung over his shoulder, he marches across the field with seven league strides, flinging out the seed in utter abandon with a mighty sweep from his powerful arm.

That is certainly a legitimate, if somewhat heroic, image for us to carry with us in our ministries in the church. We *are* called to be sowers of the Word in the field of the world, at least in our small patch of it. If we're looking for a single image to give coherence to the multi-dimensional nature of our calling, we could do worse than choose this one.

A prospective student who was inquiring about seminary informed me that one of his reasons for thinking about the ordained ministry was his perception of the pastor as the last "Renaissance man" in our society. "Jack-of-all trades" would have been a less elegant description. In any case, he saw something tremendously appealing in the variety of roles demanded of a parish pastor: teacher, preacher, scholar, counselor, prophet, priest, administrator.

In many respects that spectrum *is* inviting. It helps keep our office from being a breeding ground for boredom. Yet this very diversification can also be our despair. Unless our multiplicity of function is controlled and sustained by a single integrating purpose, our ministries and our persons begin to disintegrate.

So it may be that this vigorous figure in Jesus' parable provides such an integrating image: "Listen! A sower went out to sow." Running through our many functions is our fundamental calling to be "sowers of the Word." Whatever else we are and do, at the very center of our task is the summons to speak God's uncompromising "No!" to all human arrangements that thwart his purpose and to declare God's liberating, life-giving "Yes!" announced to us in Jesus' death and resurrection.

The sowing of this Word occurs in many modes and many places. It happens most prominently and publicly in the Sunday sermon, but also through quiet presence in a time of crisis. It occurs by way of bread placed in an out-stretched hand and in the intense listening and speaking of pastoral counseling. It can happen during a visit with an aging widow and through participation in an action program on behalf of the poor and oppressed.

This Word we sow is a word which tears down and builds up, wounds and heals, kills and makes alive. It's a word which propels the sower into places of joy and pain which she or he would never enter apart from God's command.

The vocation of the sower, therefore, is no role for what used to be called "gentleman farmers," dilettantes who prefer armchair or sideline to field and furrow and who never invest themselves in what they're doing. At least this stalwart figure in Jesus' parable presents a different picture. He tramps with steady determination through his field, sowing the seed with a fine combination of skill and abandon. He exhibits something of the force of Unamuno's words: "Sow yourself, sow the living part of yourself in the furrows of life."

* * *

There's a second place in this parable where "sowers of the Word" might be tempted to catch a reflection of their situation. It's in the soil. In fact, measured in terms of the number of words allotted to it, the soil is where the focus of the parable seems to be.

Jesus describes the farmer's field in vivid detail, especially the troublesome parts of it — the community footpath tramped hard as concrete, the sections where solid rock lies just beneath the surface, the corners overgrown with weeds and brambles. Usually this has been the part of the parable with which we've been preoccupied. All that bad soil! Twenty-five percent path, twenty-five percent rocky ground, twenty-five percent undergrowth, twenty-five percent good soil. Yet there's nothing in the parable itself to justify such a proportion. It would be a foolish farmer indeed who would waste much seed and sweat on a field as unpromising as that!

I suspect that those of us who teach and preach are largely responsible for this way of reading the parable. There are days when such an exegesis accurately reflects the view from the parsonage or office window. All that time spent preparing the seed! All that care given to its sowing! And so little to show for it! It *has* to be the soil that's at fault!

Once I was invited to participate in a retreat planned especially for pastors who had been in their ministries 20 to 25 years. Perhaps at that age pastors, as well as other middle-aged people, begin to mellow. Or it may be they'd simply become too tired to fight. Whatever the reason, I was struck by the absence among them of any sign of the common clerical disease of complaining about their congregations. They were realistic about conditions which placed their parishes a considerable distance this side of the Kingdom. They had some legitimate quarrels with their congregations. Yet, one sensed that they were "lovers' quarrels." They'd learned that if the fields they sowed and cultivated week after week and year after year weren't all good soil — well, they were far from being all bad soil either.

This is a perspective not easy to maintain. When we suddenly encounter opposition, meanness of spirit or ingratitude; when things go badly for us; when it strikes home in painful ways that the church isn't the Kingdom of God on earth, then it becomes tempting to lash out at the soil.

At such times it isn't easy to remember that the soil, no less than we who sow, belongs to and is cherished by God. We sow the Word among persons whom the Holy Spirit has already claimed in baptism and continues, in Luther's words, to "enlighten, sanctify and preserve." We live together with our people in "the holy Christian church," unholy as it sometimes will look, where God "daily forgives abundantly all my sins and the sins of all believers."

* * *

What can ultimately preserve us from cynicism and despair in our ministries, however, is neither a proper analysis of the soil nor a heroic image of ourselves as sowers. What will save us is lively confidence in the power of the seed.

Actually, this is the element in the parable on which we should focus, for it's clear that this is the point toward which Jesus is driving in telling it. The climax of the story is not the relatively small amount of seed which fails to mature or is carried away by the birds. The climax comes in Jesus' joyous announcement of what happened to the overwhelming bulk of the seed in by far the largest area of the field. There, Jesus declares, "the yield was thirtyfold, sixtyfold, and even a hundredfold."

Those who know about such matters report that tenfold was a bumper crop in that land at that time. Thirty, sixty, a hundredfold were in the realm of fantasy, way out beyond the boundaries of any farmer's imagining. It's the one truly startling, extraordinary factor in an otherwise very ordinary story.

Some say Jesus told this parable during a period in his own ministry when his sowing of the Word was going badly. It would have been easy for him to see signs of crop failure all around. People weren't listening or responding, except to oppose him. Hostile authorities lurked in the shadows. The disciples were probably taking a particularly gloomy view of the situation. To counter their despair, Jesus flings out his magnificently defiant, triumphant statement:

> *Don't be deceived by your so-called "realistic assessment of the situation" — all that rock and thorns and the birds carrying away everything they can eat. You're forgetting there's good soil there, too, and, above all, the good seed — those tiny, shrivelled up, dead-looking shells with God's own power locked up inside waiting to be released by the rain and sun — and to be released in a way that will blast all your notions of the possible!*

Perhaps lurking in the back of Jesus' mind were words of Isaiah, spoken during another time when the odds seemed all against God's purpose:

> *For as the rain and snow come down from heaven,*
>   *and return not thither but water the earth,*
> *making it bring forth and sprout,*
>   *giving seed to the sower and bread to the eater,*
> *so shall my word be that goes forth from my mouth;*
>   *it shall not return to me empty,*
> *but it shall accomplish that which I purpose,*
>   *and prosper in the thing for which I sent it.*
>   — Isaiah 55:10

Here then is the true symbol for ministry — not in the sower or the soil, but in the seed. Perhaps we should all keep one — a kernel of corn or a grain of wheat — in our studies, alongside the cross. It would remind us of that Word which, no matter how unprepossessing its form or unpromising its situation, simply will not be defeated. Neither the resistance of its hearers nor the opposition of the world nor the frailty and folly of its sowers can finally undo it.

One difficulty is that those of us who sow won't be there at harvest time to see the final proof of that promise. It's always seed time in our ministries of the Word. But we sow in confidence and hope, because, in the words of the chief Sower of the Seed: "... unless a grain of wheat falls into the earth and dies it remains alone; but if it dies, it bears much fruit" (John 12:24).

He was speaking, of course, about the seed of his own life. He sowed it at last on a hill. It burst into blossom in a garden. And it has born fruit a millionfold in all times and in all places, including our own.

Christ's Militia
Ephesians 6:10-17

During the late summer of 1992, the noise of battle was again heard in the countryside around Gettysburg — only this time without casualties. Armies of reenactment soldiers fired guns without bullets as part of the filming of Michael Sharra's prizewinning novel, *The Killer Angels.*

That title, which was the nickname of a Maine regiment which fought gallantly at Gettysburg, has always intrigued me. It marries two normally incompatible words: "killer," with its images of brutality and death, and "angels," with its associations of gentleness and care. Yet this odd combination of words could very well serve as a designation for the church.

Christians in New Testament times might not have been startled by such a suggestion. In John's visionary battle scenes in the book of Revelation, actual "killer angels" seem to be everywhere. And, in spite of the fact that many of the first Christians were pacifists, they delighted in referring to themselves as *militia Christi* — "Christ's Militia." They called their baptism a *sacramentum,* the term Roman legionnaires used for the oath of loyalty they swore to the emperor. Even so, Christians saw themselves as inductees, by baptism, into the army of the Lord, there to follow Christ, their captain, into battle against the hosts of evil.

It's in this vein that the author of Ephesians describes Christians as though they were dressed in the battle gear of a Roman soldier. They wear "the breastplate of righteousness" and "the helmet of salvation." They carry in one hand "the shield of faith," and, in the other, "the sword of the Spirit," which is the Word of God.

We follow the same tradition when we join in singing Luther's great "Battle Hymn Of The Reformation," in which you can almost hear the thunder of cannon and the marching of armies. Even though, as the church in this late twentieth century, we may not always *feel* like an army or *look* like an army or *act* like an army, through the sacrament of our baptism, "Christ's Militia" is what we've been called to be.

* * *

To see ourselves in this way is, among other things, a strong reminder that *the church is mission.*

It's impossible to think of an army without a mission. No army fulfills its reason for being by its life in the camp.

I once read about a fort the British built in India during the colonial period. They located it at a strategic crossroad in the center of a frontier city, so that they'd be poised to repulse any invading enemy. Years passed, decades passed, and no enemy came. All that time, in true British fashion, the fort and its regiment were maintained in A-1 condition. The flag was raised at sunrise and lowered at sunset, the band played, the troops paraded. And then one day an enemy struck. Unfortunately, by this time the city had grown away from the fort. The fort was no longer situated at a strategic crossroad. The beautifully drilled troops were useless, and the city fell. At some point during those decades, the regiment had lost its mission.

The parable for the church is clear. We aren't a drill team or a color guard but an army with a mission. And that mission doesn't lie "inside the fort," where we perform the tasks of maintaining our property, perfecting our rituals of worship and nurturing and supporting one another in our common life. Important as these tasks are, our real mission as "Christ's Militia" lies "outside the fort" in the world God made and loves and into which God dispatches us on assignments of truth, justice and healing. Or, as the writer of Ephesians puts it, we're sent out to fight not "against enemies of flesh and blood ... but against the cosmic powers of this present darkness."

When we begin to think of the church in this way, a second thing becomes clear: *It's the laity who are the spearhead of the church's mission in and to the world.*

Not the clergy, but the laity. The service of pastors and others called to full time offices in the church is primarily "inside the fort" — teaching and preaching, administering the sacraments, ministering to the laity when they return from the front. Our special vocation is to serve the rest of the people of God in such a way that they'll always be "combat ready" for their places of service in the world.

Of course, the laity also have important tasks "inside the fort." No unit of Christ's army can function without volunteers who teach and sing and lead and give and perform the dozens of other tasks needed within a congregation.

But here, inside the structures of the church, is not the primary place the laity are called to serve. That place is "outside the walls," in households and neighborhoods, in offices and schoolrooms, in factories and laboratories, in volunteer agencies and political parties — all those places that command their time and consume their energy six days of the week.

Just how easy it is for us to forget that was brought home to me a few years ago when I was asked to organize a panel discussion on "Religion and Politics." Someone suggested we invite as a panelist an active Christian layman in our city who was a lawyer, a member of the school board and active in local politics. He seemed just the person to bring these often separated worlds together.

A few nights before the meeting, I called him to ask what I should say in introducing him, and his reply went something like this: "Well, it's true that I'm active in politics and am serving on the school board, but you needn't mention that. What I'm really proud of is the fact that I've represented my church three times at its national convention."

I hung up the phone saddened — saddened because his church had never helped this faithful layman see that what he did day after day in his law office, in the heated meetings of the school board and in the caucuses of his political party was just as much — and I would argue *more strategically* — his service of God than his activity in the internal life of the church.

He would have been helped by hearing bold words Luther once spoke: "The housemaid on her knees scrubbing the floor is doing a work as pleasing in the eyes of Almighty God as the priest on his knees before the altar saying the mass."[1] To get the full impact of those words we need to update Luther's categories:
- the bank clerk at her window cashing a check as the church council member counting Sunday's offering;
- the public school teacher instructing a science class as the church school teacher with a class of ten-year-olds;
- the staff member of a soup kitchen as a pastor administering the bread and wine.

Ever since God became incarnate in a village carpenter, what we call "ordinary" has been touched with extraordinary significance. Surely Jesus crafted ox yokes and house doors with the same care he later devoted to creating parables, and he would have seen both as the calling under God for which he bore responsibility and with which God was well pleased.

I once heard about another layman who understood that. He was riding on a train beside an aggressive Christian who asked him, "And what do you do to serve the Lord?" Without a moment's hesitation, he replied, "I bake bread!"

He'd come to understand that serving Christ, for him, meant baking an honest loaf and selling it at an honest price, paying fair wages and providing good working conditions for his employees, being straightforward in his advertising and in his dealings with his competitors. In a way, he'd transformed his bakery into a temple; his ovens had become an altar; he'd made his daily work his offering to God through his service of his neighbor. He was "Christ's soldier" at the front.

And so are all the people we're privileged to serve — "Killer Angels" deployed daily not on missions of aggression but errands of compassion and justice. Indeed, all of us together are members of "Christ's Militia," incorporated into his army by baptism and assigned by him to our various duty stations. Some, like ourselves, serve primarily at the base, equipping others for their mission in the world and ministering to them when they return. The church's rhythm of gathering and scattering goes on and on. Each phase is essential to *God's* mission and each assignment is worthy of the best we and our people can bring to it.

---

1. Martin Luther. Source unknown.

www.ingramcontent.com/pod-product-compliance
Lightning Source LLC
Chambersburg PA
CBHW071753040426
42446CB00012B/2538